New York
a Dutch Co

Janey Levy

ROSEN CLASSROOM

PRIMARYSOURCE

Rosen Classroom Books & Materials

New York

Published in 2003 by The Rosen Publishing Group, Inc.
29 East 21st Street, New York, NY 10010

Book Design: Haley Wilson

ISBN: 0-8239-8403-6
6-pack ISBN: 0-8239-8416-8

Contents

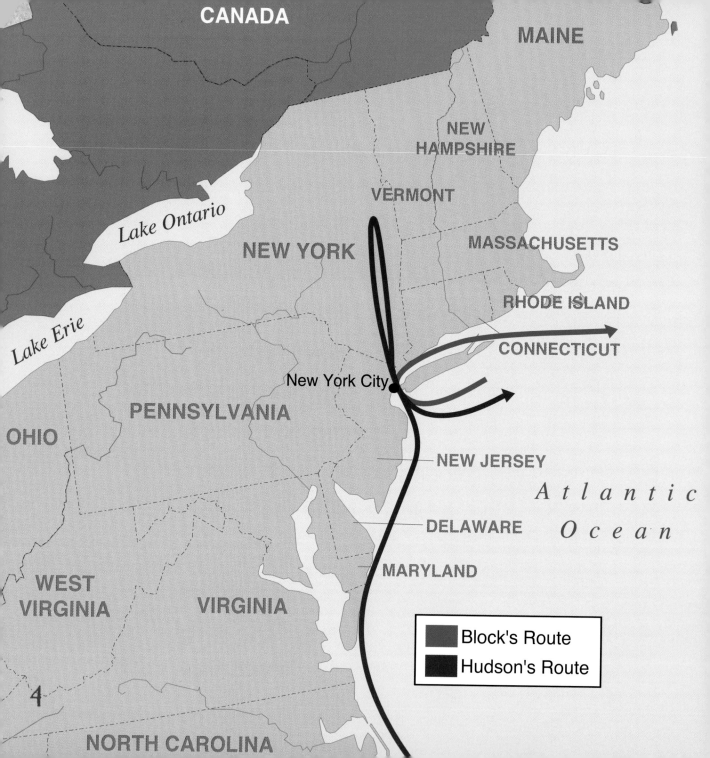

CANADA

MAINE

NEW HAMPSHIRE

VERMONT

Lake Ontario

NEW YORK

MASSACHUSETTS

RHODE ISLAND

CONNECTICUT

Lake Erie

New York City

PENNSYLVANIA

OHIO

NEW JERSEY

Atlantic Ocean

DELAWARE

MARYLAND

WEST VIRGINIA

VIRGINIA

4

NORTH CAROLINA

Block's Route
Hudson's Route

Dutch Explorers in New York

The Netherlands was one of the most powerful countries in Europe in the 1600s. Dutch people worked hard and had money to spend. They wanted a share of the **New World's** riches. Some Dutch merchants hired English sea captain Henry Hudson, who explored the areas now called New York Harbor and the Hudson River in 1609 and claimed them for the Netherlands.

In 1613, Dutch merchants hired Adriaen Block to explore the areas Hudson had visited. Fire destroyed Block's ship in New York Harbor. He and his crew built the first Dutch settlement on Manhattan Island and lived there while they built a new ship.

◄ Block traded with Native Americans for beaver furs, which the Dutch valued. The areas Block explored were home to several groups of Native Americans, who lived in villages much like the one shown in the small picture above.

6

Dutch Colonists Arrive

Block called the area he explored New Netherland. Some Dutch people who heard about New Netherland decided to go there. In 1624, the first colonists set up trading posts in New York Harbor, on the Connecticut River, and on the Hudson River at Fort Orange, near what is now Albany.

In 1626, a war between the **Algonquian** and the **Iroquois** put the Fort Orange colonists in danger. Peter Minuit, the colony leader, moved the colonists to Manhattan to keep them safe. They founded the village of New Amsterdam at the tip of Manhattan Island on land Minuit had purchased from the Algonquian.

◀ This color drawing of New Amsterdam from around 1670 shows ships peacefully sailing in the harbor. Houses fill the growing city. A windmill for grinding grain appears at the left of the picture. The large building to the right of the windmill is a church.

NIEU AMSTERDAM

Cum Privilegio Ordinum Hollandiæ et West-Frisiæ

8

The Dutch West India Company

The Dutch government established the Dutch West India Company in 1621 to help New Netherland grow. The fur trade brought the company great wealth, but the colony needed more settlers.

To draw people to the colony, the company set up the **patroon** system in 1629. Each patroon received a large area of land. In return, the patroon paid for fifty people to go to the colony. These colonists lived on the patroon's land and raised crops for him. The company also established its own farms in the colony. African **slaves** were forced to work on these farms.

Around 1645, Isaac Joques wrote a book about life in New Netherland. The pages shown above come from a copy of the book printed in 1862. The picture to the left shows Dutch colonists outside New Amsterdam holding the crops that made them wealthy. Behind them, African slaves are working.

9

Beschrijvinghe

Van

VIRGINIA,

Nieuw Nederlandt,

Nieuw Engelandt,

En d'Eylanden

BERMUDES,

Berbados, en S. Christoffel.

Dienstelijck voor elck een derwaerts handelende, en alle voort-planters van nieuw Colonien.

Met kopere Figuren verciert.

MYN GLAS LOOPT RAS

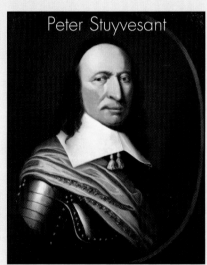

Peter Stuyvesant

t' AMSTERDAM,

By JOOST HARTGERS, Boeck-verkooper op den Dam, besyden 't Stadt-huys, op de hoeck vande Kalver-straet, inde Boeck-winckel, Anno 1651.

New Netherland's Government

The Dutch West India Company wanted a leader who would run the colony so the company would make money. In 1638, they sent a man named Willem Kieft to govern New Netherland. In 1639, Kieft tried to tax Native Americans in the area to increase profits for the company. This made the Native Americans angry and led to a war. The colonists won the war in 1645, but many complained that Kieft was a bad leader.

In 1647, the company sent Peter Stuyvesant to be the new leader of the colony. The rules Stuyvesant made for the colonists brought peace to New Netherland. Life in the colony improved, but Stuyvesant's rules were stern and most colonists did not like him.

◀ Books like the one shown here—titled *Description of Virginia, New Netherland, New England*—helped spread the news about the better life Stuyvesant brought to New Netherland. This made people from many different countries want to live in the colony.

Family Life in New Netherland

The Dutch believed that a country's well-being depended on healthy, happy families. In a proper family, the father's job was to earn money. The mother's job was to keep the home clean and orderly. Cleanliness was especially important to the Dutch.

Children were the center of Dutch family life. Both parents took part in raising the children and preparing them for life as adults. However, Peter Stuyvesant believed most New Netherland colonists spoiled their children. He did not approve of the amount of attention parents gave their children.

◀ Family life was very important to the Dutch colonists. This painting by Dutch artist Pieter de Hooch shows a mother and child in a clean Dutch home. The mother is working, while the child appears to be playing. Both seem to be happy.

Homes in New Netherland

The first colonists had to build houses quickly. The earliest homes were made of mud and bark, and usually had only one room. Once land had been cleared for farming and crops had been planted, the colonists had time to build larger homes of wood. These homes usually had steep roofs, like **traditional** Dutch houses.

Around 1650, wealthy colonists began to build

houses of brick similar to those back in the Netherlands. In towns like New Amsterdam, the houses were narrow and close together. Inside were just a few pieces of simple wooden furniture.

◀ This Dutch wood house was built on Long Island in 1661. Shown above is the living room of a Dutch house in what is now Tarrytown, New York. Large fireplaces like the one here provided heat for the home.

Farming in New Netherland

By 1660, farming had replaced the fur trade as the most important work in the colony. Farmers grew crops that were grown back in the Netherlands, like wheat, **rye**, apples, cabbages, carrots, and spinach. They also raised cows, goats, sheep, and hogs they had brought with them from the Netherlands. The Native Americans taught the colonists how to grow crops like squash, pumpkins, tobacco, and corn.

Traditional Dutch tools made farm work easier. The Dutch plow dug deep rows in the dirt and made planting easier. The Dutch wagon hauled tools and grain during the week. On Sunday, it carried the family to church.

◀ To grind grains like wheat, rye, and corn, the colonists built windmills like the one shown here. This etching was created in 1641 by a famous Dutch painter named Rembrandt van Rijn.

Learning and Playing

Boys and girls in the Dutch colony learned to read and write. Boys also learned a craft, such as building furniture or wagons, making glass, or printing books. Girls learned from their mothers how to cook, **spin** thread, make clothes, and keep the home clean. All children learned about religion and how to be good members of the community.

When they had time, the colonists played many of the games and sports that were popular in the Netherlands. These included ice skating, sledding, and *kolven* (GOHL-fen), a game that used a curved stick to hit a ball. *Kolven* could be played on grass in the summer, like golf, or on ice in the winter, like hockey.

◀ Another popular Dutch game was skittle. It was a form of bowling played outdoors on the grass. A wooden ball was used to knock down wooden pins.

HONI SOIT QVI MAL Y PENS

20

The End of the Dutch Colony

By the early 1600s, British colonies surrounded New Netherland. Britain's king, Charles II, wanted to add New Netherland to his colonies because of its successful fur trade and good farmland. In 1664, Charles told his brother James, **duke** of York, that he could be the ruler of New Netherland. James sent nearly 2,000 soldiers to take control of his new colony.

Stuyvesant wanted to fight the British, but he had fewer than 150 soldiers. The Dutch colonists had been unhappy with Stuyvesant's stern rules for many years and were not willing to fight for him. Stuyvesant was forced to **surrender** the colony. He left with his soldiers and returned to the Netherlands.

◄ This picture shows James in the fancy and expensive clothes worn at the British court. In the upper right corner is the royal coat of arms, with the official motto, or saying, "Evil to him who evil thinks." When Charles II died in 1685, James became King James II.

Dutch Life in the British Colony

The British renamed the colony New York. New Amsterdam became New York City. Except for these changes, the British allowed the Dutch colonists to continue their lives as before. Everyone who wanted to stay was allowed to. The colonists could keep their land, their houses, and their personal property. They could continue to speak Dutch, follow their religion, and practice their traditions.

Because the new British rulers made these wise decisions, most of the Dutch colonists stayed. Peter Stuyvesant even returned in 1668. The colony continued to grow. Many of the Dutch ways of doing things became lasting parts of life in the colonies.

Glossary

Algonquian (al-GAHN-kwee-uhn) The name given to several groups of Native Americans in the northeast who spoke Algonquian languages.

duke (DOOK) A European noble.

Iroquois (EAR-uh-kwoy) The name given to several groups of Native Americans in the northeast who spoke Iroquois languages.

New World (NOO WUHRLD) A name given to all of North America, Central America, and South America by European explorers.

patroon (puh-TROON) A wealthy man given control of a large area of land in the New World by the Dutch government.

rye (RI) A grain that is used to make flour or to feed farm animals.

slave (SLAYV) A person who is "owned" by and forced to work for another person.

spin (SPIN) To draw out and twist fiber into thread.

surrender (suh-REHN-dur) To give up power to someone else.

traditional (truh-DIH-shuh-nuhl) The way something has been done or made by a group of people for a long time.

Index

Primary Source List

Page 5. Native American Settlement. Hand-colored engraving by Theodor de Bry from Thomas Hariot's *A Briefe and True Report of the New Found Land of Virginia*, 1588. Based on watercolor by John White, 1585–1587.

Page 6. *New Amsterdam, now New York, on the Island of Manhattan*. Color drawing, ca. 1670, now in the Royal Archives in The Hague. Based on watercolor, ca. 1650, now in the Austria National Library.

Page 8. *New Amsterdam*. Etching, ca. 1650. The etching can be found in the I. N. Phelps Stokes Collection, Miriam and Ira D. Wallach Division of Art, Prints and Photographs, The New York Public Library.

Page 9. Pages from *Novum Belgium*. Manuscript by Isaac Joques, ca. 1645. Published in New York by Presse Cramoisy de J. M. Shea, 1862.

Page 10. Title page, *Description of Virginia, New Netherland, New England*. By Joost Hartgers, 1651.

Page 10 (inset). Portrait of Peter Stuyvesant. Painting by Henri Couturier, ca. 1660–1663. Now in the New-York Historical Society.

Page 12. *The Bedroom*. Painting by Pieter de Hooch, ca. 1660. Now in the National Gallery of Art, Washington, D.C.

Page 14. Bowne House. Built by John Bowne, 1661; in Flushing, Queens, New York.

Page 15. Seventeenth century–style Dutch chamber in the Van Cortland Museum, the Bronx. The museum was originally the home of Frederick Van Cortland, who built it in 1748.

Page 16. *The Windmill*. Etching by Rembrandt van Rijn, 1641.

Page 18. *Skittle Players Outside an Inn*. Painting by Jan Steen, ca. 1660. Now in the National Gallery, London.

Page 20. Portrait of James, duke of York. Engraving, ca. 1670.

Web Sites

Due to the changing nature of Internet links, The Rosen Publishing Group, Inc. has developed an on-line list of Web sites related to the subjects of this book. This site is updated regularly. Please use this link to access the list:
http://www.rcbmlinks.com/nysh/nydc/